CIVIL RIGHTS HEROES

Thurgood Marshall

By Amy B. Rogers

New York

Published in 2022 by Cavendish Square Publishing, LLC
29 E. 21st Street, New York, NY 10010

Copyright © 2022 by Cavendish Square Publishing, LLC

First Edition

No part of this publication may be reproduced, stored in a retrieval system, or transmitted in any form or by any means—electronic, mechanical, photocopying, recording, or otherwise—without the prior permission of the copyright owner. Request for permission should be addressed to Permissions, Cavendish Square Publishing, 29 E. 21st Street, New York, NY 10010. Tel (877) 980-4450; fax (877) 980-4454.

Website: cavendishsq.com

This publication represents the opinions and views of the author based on his or her personal experience, knowledge, and research. The information in this book serves as a general guide only. The author and publisher have used their best efforts in preparing this book and disclaim liability rising directly or indirectly from the use and application of this book.

All websites were available and accurate when this book was sent to press.

Portions of this work were originally authored by Barbara M. Linde and published as *Thurgood Marshall* (*Civil Rights Crusaders*). All new material this edition authored by Amy B. Rogers.

Library of Congress Cataloging-in-Publication Data
Names: Rogers, Amy B., author.
Title: Thurgood Marshall / Amy B. Rogers.
Description: New York : Cavendish Square Publishing, [2022] | Series: The inside guide. Civil rights heroes | Includes index.
Identifiers: LCCN 2020029738 | ISBN 9781502660206 (library binding) | ISBN 9781502660183 (paperback) | ISBN 9781502660190 (set) | ISBN 9781502660213 (ebook)
Subjects: LCSH: Marshall, Thurgood, 1908-1993–Juvenile literature. | African American judges–Biography–Juvenile literature. | United States. Supreme Court–Officials and employees–Biography–Juvenile literature.
Classification: LCC KF8745.M34 R639 2022 | DDC 347.73/2634 [B]–dc23
LC record available at https://lccn.loc.gov/2020029738

Editor: Katie Kawa
Copy Editor: Abby Young
Designer: Andrea Davison-Bartolotta

The photographs in this book are used by permission and through the courtesy of: Cover, pp. 4, 22 Hank Walker/The LIFE Picture Collection via Getty Images; pp. 6, 7, 13, 15, 16, 19, 21, 29 (bottom) Bettmann/Getty Images; p. 8 Corbis Historical/Getty Images; p. 9 Mandel Ngan/AFP via Getty Images; pp. 10, 28 (top left) Library of Congress/Corbis/VCG via Getty Images; p. 12 rdegrie/E+/Getty Images; p. 14 Westend61/Getty Images; p. 18 Robert W. Kelley/The LIFE Picture Collection via Getty Images; p. 20 Carl Iwasaki/The LIFE Images Collection via Getty Images; p. 24 Bachrach/Getty Images; p. 25 Cornell Capa/The LIFE Picture Collection via Getty Images; pp. 26, 27 Cheriss May/NurPhoto via Getty Images; p. 28 (bottom left) Stan Wayman/The LIFE Picture Collection via Getty Images; p. 28 (bottom right) Daniel Acker/Bloomberg via Getty Images; p. 28 (top right) Keystone/Getty Images; p. 29 (top) Walter Bibikow/Stone/Getty Images.

Some of the images in this book illustrate individuals who are models. The depictions do not imply actual situations or events.

CPSIA compliance information: Batch #CS22CSQ: For further information contact Cavendish Square Publishing LLC, New York, New York, at 1-877-980-4450.

Printed in the United States of America

CONTENTS

Chapter One — 5
Change Through the Courts

Chapter Two — 11
A Lawyer's Life

Chapter Three — 17
The Path to the Supreme Court

Chapter Four — 23
Fighting in His Own Way

Timeline — 28

Think About It! — 29

Glossary — 30

Find Out More — 31

Index — 32

Thurgood Marshall fought hard to change laws that he believed were unfair and unjust.

CHANGE THROUGH THE COURTS

Chapter One

Everyone has their own **unique** skills, interests, and ideas that they can use to make the world a better place. During the civil rights movement, which reached its peak in the 1950s and 1960s, leaders used many different methods to fight for equality for Black Americans. Some made speeches to inspire people. Some led marches and other kinds of protests. Thurgood Marshall became famous for fighting for equality through the courts. By changing laws, he changed the country.

Stopping Segregation

Thurgood and other leaders in the civil rights movement worked to end segregation in the United States. Segregation was the forced separation of Black Americans and white Americans. Black Americans were forced to use separate bathrooms, water fountains, and other facilities. Schools were often segregated too.

Fast Fact

In 1896, the U.S. Supreme Court made an important decision in the case of *Plessy v. Ferguson*. It said that segregation could be legal as long as the separate facilities were equal in quality. However, facilities for Black Americans were often worse than those for white Americans.

Segregation was legal in many parts of the United States, especially in the South. This was because of laws called Jim Crow laws, which allowed for legal discrimination, or unfair treatment, against Black Americans.

Legal segregation lasted for almost 100 years in the American South. Thurgood and many other Black leaders spent much of their lives trying to end it.

Breaking Through with *Brown*

Thurgood used the U.S. court system to fight segregation, often arguing his cases before the Supreme Court—the highest court in the United States. The most famous case he argued before the Supreme Court was

Brown v. Board of Education of Topeka. Thurgood used this case to argue that school segregation was unconstitutional, or against the U.S. Constitution. In a groundbreaking decision, the Supreme Court agreed with Thurgood.

Thurgood's victory in this case helped inspire other civil rights leaders to stand up against segregation in their own ways. He helped push the civil rights movement forward.

Fast Fact
The Supreme Court's ruling on *Brown v. Board of Education of Topeka* happened in 1954.

An Important First

Thurgood wasn't just a **role model** because of his work arguing cases before the Supreme Court. He was also a role model because he eventually served on the Supreme Court himself. In 1967, Thurgood became the first African American Supreme Court justice.

As a Supreme Court justice, Thurgood was able to interpret laws and the Constitution to push for greater justice and equality in the United States.

Thurgood continued to fight for the rights of all people as a Supreme Court justice.

THE SUPREME COURT

The U.S. Constitution set up a government with three branches. The legislative branch—Congress—makes the laws. The executive branch—the president, vice president, and **cabinet**—enforces the laws. The judicial branch, which is made up of the Supreme Court and lower courts, interprets the laws.

The Supreme Court's job is to decide if laws are unconstitutional, which means they go against the Constitution. They have to apply the words of the Constitution to a world the Founding Fathers never could have imagined. It's not an easy job, but it's an important one.

Fast Fact

Judges on the Supreme Court are known as justices. There is typically one chief justice and eight associate justices serving on the court at all times. Justices serve for life or until they decide to retire.

The Supreme Court typically has nine members, and for almost 200 years, those members were all white men. Thurgood's appointment changed this. The makeup of the Supreme Court changed again in 1981 when Sandra Day O'Connor (*center*) became the first woman to serve as a justice.

The Work Continues

Thurgood once said, "A child born to a Black mother in a state like Mississippi … has exactly the same rights as a white baby born to the wealthiest person in the United States. It's not true, but I challenge anyone to say it is not a goal worth working for." Thurgood knew that **racism** kept Black people from being given the same rights as white people, and he spent his life working toward the goal of changing that.

Today, that work continues. By working to change unfair laws and create ones that protect all Americans, people are keeping Thurgood's **legacy** alive.

The courts are still seen as a powerful tool for creating change. The Supreme Court continues to rule on many cases involving equal rights for different groups of Americans, including **LGBTQ+** Americans, women, and Black Americans.

Thurgood Marshall's family liked to debate important issues. He said this helped him train for a future as a lawyer.

A LAWYER'S LIFE

Chapter Two

Thurgood Marshall was born on July 2, 1908, in Baltimore, Maryland. When he was born, his parents named him Thoroughgood, but he decided to shorten his name when he was in elementary school. Thurgood was encouraged to think for himself while he was growing up. He developed strong opinions on everything from his name to the problems he saw in the world around him.

A Father's Influence

Thurgood's father, William Marshall, shaped his future in important ways. William liked to take his sons to court to watch the lawyers at work. He would then encourage his sons to debate about the cases and make strong arguments. This gave Thurgood the skills he would use later in life as a lawyer and Supreme Court justice. In Thurgood's words, William "never told me to become a lawyer, he turned me into one."

Thurgood also developed a strong understanding of the U.S. Constitution from a young age. This was because he had to read the Constitution as a punishment in high school.

Fast Fact
Thurgood's great-grandfather had been enslaved in Maryland.

Shown here is a copy of the U.S. Constitution. After Thurgood was forced to read it as a punishment, he learned how important it was. He then memorized it!

Law School

After high school, Thurgood went to Lincoln University in Pennsylvania. He knew he wanted to be a lawyer, so he then started applying to law schools. He wanted to go to the University of Maryland, but he wasn't accepted because the school was only for white students at the time.

Thurgood decided to go to law school at Howard University in Washington, D.C. While he was at Howard, he met the man who would become his **mentor**, Charles Hamilton Houston. Charles believed in fighting for equality using the courts. He taught Thurgood to see that laws can be a powerful tool to create social change, such as ending segregation.

Fast Fact

Thurgood married Vivian "Buster" Burey in 1929. They were married until she died in February 1955. He married Cecilia Suyat in December 1955.

Shown here is Charles Hamilton Houston. Thurgood once said, "Charlie Houston insisted that we be social engineers rather than lawyers." This meant he taught his students to use the law to engineer, or create, social change.

An Important Case

After graduating from law school, Thurgood began working as a lawyer in Baltimore. He kept in touch with Charles, who was working as a lawyer for the National Association for the Advancement of Colored People (NAACP). This organization was founded in 1909 to fight for civil rights for Black Americans.

Thurgood and Charles worked together on a case in 1935. In *Murray v. Pearson*, they argued that it was unconstitutional for the University of Maryland to keep a Black student from attending because of his race. They won the case, and the school that had rejected Thurgood for being Black was soon **integrated**.

HOWARD UNIVERSITY

Howard University has existed since 1867. It has always been open to students of any race, but it was set up to offer Black Americans an opportunity to get a college education. It has a large library of African American history and offers classes in a wide variety of subjects—from medicine and law to communications and education.

Howard is part of a group of schools in the United States known as historically Black colleges and universities (HBCUs). Other HBCUs include Spelman College in Atlanta, Georgia, and Hampton University in Hampton, Virginia.

Other famous Americans who attended Howard University (*shown here*) include Vice President Kamala Harris, author Toni Morrison, and actors Anthony Anderson, Taraji P. Henson, and Chadwick Boseman.

Working for the NAACP

Thurgood soon left his private practice and began working for the NAACP full-time. He took on more cases involving segregation in colleges and universities. He also argued cases that dealt with voting rights, housing discrimination, and other civil rights issues. Thurgood sometimes took these cases to the Supreme Court.

Thurgood argued these cases as the head of the NAACP's Legal Defense and Educational Fund. He set up this part of the NAACP in 1940 to specifically take on cases that could lead to the overturning of segregation laws. Thurgood had his sights set on ending segregation across the country.

Fast Fact

Thurgood won his first Supreme Court case in 1940. During his time with the NAACP, he won 29 of the 32 cases he argued before the nation's highest court.

Thurgood spent his early legal career working toward challenging school segregation in the Supreme Court.

Thurgood's most important Supreme Court victory came in the case *Brown v. Board of Education of Topeka*. He's shown in the center of this photo with other lawyers who helped him argue against school segregation.

CORETTA TAKING CHARGE

Chapter Three

Coretta became one of the most well-known women of the civil rights movement and spoke out about the need to include more women in the movement. She supported her husband, but when she suddenly found herself without him, she also became a leader on her own.

Tough Times

Coretta spent much of the early days of the civil rights movement standing by Martin's side as he directed others and helped lead the movement in the South. Martin's work and Coretta's support of it sometimes put their lives in danger. In fact, their house was bombed in 1956 when Coretta was home with their daughter Yolanda. Coretta was lucky to be alive, but she didn't let this act of violence stop her from supporting her husband and standing by his side.

Fast Fact

Coretta planned and took part in "Freedom Concerts." These events raised money for the Southern Christian Leadership Conference—a civil rights group.

"Freedom Concerts," like this one in 1963, allowed people to come together for a good cause and enjoy music from popular performers.

Traveling

Coretta and Martin became popular figures. They traveled the world, sometimes together but sometimes apart. Coretta was often seen marching next to her husband at important protests during the civil rights movement. At other times, she watched the children while Martin traveled.

Coretta's Beliefs

Coretta had her own voice and her own beliefs. She was very much against war and for peace. Unlike Martin, Coretta spoke out early about her feelings toward a war that was starting in Vietnam. Later, she was asked to take part in international peace talks and events, such as the Women's Strike for Peace. She joined the Women's International League for Peace and Freedom in 1968. She also gave speeches when Martin couldn't.

Coretta joined her husband for marches and at other public events.

Martin's Death

On April 4, 1968, Coretta's world was turned upside down. That day, Martin was assassinated, or killed, at a motel in Memphis, Tennessee. Coretta was **devastated**, but she wouldn't let his death

Fast Fact

The Women's Strike for Peace was a worldwide event protesting **nuclear testing**. It happened on November 1, 1961.

stop her from working. Days after the tragedy, Coretta led and spoke at a march that Martin was supposed to join. Later, she spoke at the Lincoln Memorial in Washington, D.C., as part of the Poor People's Campaign. These actions made people respect Coretta for the activist she was. It also turned her into a new leader for the civil rights movement.

Coretta spoke at different gatherings, such as this one for the Poor People's Campaign in Washington, D.C., in 1968.

Taking Martin's Place

Coretta believed the country needed to change. At first, she used parts of Martin's famous speeches about racial equality when she spoke. Then, she figured out

Fast Fact

Other leaders were also killed in the 1960s, including activist Malcolm X and President John F. Kennedy.

her own message—she wanted everyone to be equal. Coretta spent the rest of her life working for civil rights for all, especially women. She kept Martin's **legacy** alive while also creating her own.

Coretta is shown here with her daughter Bernice at Martin's funeral in 1968. Coretta knew it was her job to keep her husband's legacy alive after his death.

THE CIVIL RIGHTS ACT

The civil rights movement led to real changes for Black Americans. The Civil Rights Act of 1964 made it illegal to discriminate against anyone based on race, beliefs, or whether they are a man or a woman. This also ended segregation in public places. This was an important step in the history of the civil rights movement. Martin, Coretta, and other activists worked hard to get the Civil Rights Act passed. The work of Martin, Coretta, and other activists also led to another important act, called the Voting Rights Act of 1965. This act stopped practices that kept Black people from voting.

Coretta continued helping others as she got older.

A LIFE WELL LIVED

Chapter Four

Coretta made a decision to carry on Martin's dreams and mission. She did this in many ways: by writing books about her life with him, starting organizations devoted to his causes, and delivering speeches all over the world. However, she did more than just make sure people remembered Martin; she made sure they remembered her too.

Remembering Martin

In 1968, months after Martin died, Coretta started the Martin Luther King Jr. Center for Nonviolent Social Change in Atlanta. Today, it's known as the King Center. It educates people about taking peaceful actions during difficult times and about social justice. In 1969, Coretta published a book called *My Life with Martin Luther King, Jr.* In January 1986, she accomplished another goal of hers—to make Martin's birthday a national holiday.

Fast Fact
In 2017, Coretta's last book was published posthumously, or after she died. It's called *Coretta: My Life, My Love, My Legacy.*

The King Center in Atlanta is shown here.

Her Own Work

Coretta also spent a lot of time working for equality for all. She believed all people deserved to be treated the same, no matter who they were or where they came from. She cared especially about equal rights for women and groups such as the poor and the LGBTQ+ community. In the 1990s, she voiced support for the LGBTQ+ community, hoping that one day everyone could live in a world in which people loved and supported each other.

Fast Fact

Martin Luther King Jr. Day is celebrated on the third Monday in January. People all around the country volunteer or attend events.

Coretta believed that women everywhere should be treated the same as men.

ENJOYING THE ARTS

Two prizes, one for authors and one for illustrators, are carrying on Coretta Scott King's name and legacy today. The Coretta Scott King Awards honor one African American author and one African American illustrator who've captured the African American experience in their work. Books selected focus on either young adult or children's audiences. The award for authors started in 1969, and the illustration award began in 1974. The 2020 award winner for authors was *New Kid* by Jerry Craft. That same year, *The Undefeated*, illustrated by Kadir Nelson, won the illustration award.

Coretta helped form many groups that fought for equality, including the Full Employment Action Council in 1974 to fight for jobs for the unemployed. She also met with peacemakers from all over the world, including presidents and other political leaders.

A Voice for Others

Coretta also stood up for the rights of people in other countries. For example, for many years in South Africa, there was another type of segregation

Every public place in South Africa was separated, including public benches.

happening called apartheid. This had been going on for decades, but an anti-apartheid movement was gaining more support in the 1980s. People in South African towns lived, worked, and played in areas separated by race. Coretta thought this segregation was wrong. She protested against it and was arrested.

> **Fast Fact**
> One of the biggest leaders against apartheid was Nelson Mandela. He was a South African activist who became the country's president.

A Long, Full Life

As she grew older, Coretta became more active in other issues in the United States. She spoke about civil rights and about economic issues. She also toured the country, wrote more books, and protected Martin's legacy. Above all, she continued to work hard. She died on January 30, 2006, having lived a full life working for justice. Today, the King family still continues the work of Coretta and Martin.

TIMELINE

In Coretta's Life | In the World

1927
Coretta Scott is born on April 27.

1929
The Great Depression starts.

1953
Coretta marries Martin Luther King Jr. on June 18.

1963
John F. Kennedy is assassinated.

1964
The Civil Rights Act passes.

1968
Martin is assassinated on April 4.

1969
My Life with Martin Luther King, Jr. is published.

1986
Martin Luther King Jr. Day becomes a national holiday.

2001
The September 11 terrorist attacks occur.

2006
Coretta Scott King dies on January 30.

THINK ABOUT IT!

1. Why are civil rights important in a society? What groups have had to fight for civil rights throughout history?

2. Think about Coretta's and Martin's approaches to social change. Do you think their message of nonviolence was the right way to bring change? Why or why not?

3. What changes do you think are needed in society today? How could you help start your own movement?

4. Did Coretta's story inspire you? What can you learn from her about making the world a better place for all people?

GLOSSARY

activist: A person who works to bring change in the world.

boycott: The act of refusing to have dealings with a person or business in order to force change.

civil right: A freedom granted to people by law.

devastate: To deeply sadden.

discriminate: To treat people differently because of race or beliefs.

entrepreneur: A person starting a business.

Freedom Rider: A person who traveled on buses to different states in the South in the 1960s, trying to change segregation laws dealing with buses and bus stations.

legacy: The memory or work of a person after they've died.

LGBTQ+: Relating to a group made up of people who see themselves as a gender different from the sex they were assigned at birth or who want to be in romantic relationships that aren't only male-female. LGBTQ stands for lesbian, gay, bisexual, transgender, and queer or questioning.

nuclear testing: The practice of dropping very powerful bombs in desert areas; these took place between the 1940s and 1970s.

stereotype: A way of thinking about a person or group of people based on certain characteristics or habits; stereotypes aren't always accurate and can be harmful.

FIND OUT MORE

Books

Calkhoven, Laurie. *Martin Luther King Jr.* New York, NY: DK, 2019.

Herman, Gail. *Who Was Coretta Scott King?* New York, NY: Penguin, 2017.

Hooks, Gwendolyn. *If You Were a Kid During the Civil Rights Movement.* New York, NY: Children's Press, 2017.

Websites

Civil Rights Movement
kids.britannica.com/kids/article/civil-rights-movement/403522
This website explores key moments and actions in the civil rights movement and includes a slideshow of historic photographs.

Fun Facts from Black History: Coretta Scott King
www.youtube.com/watch?v=Mr3P9vVo-ao
This short animated video for students explores the biography of Coretta Scott King.

Hero for All: Martin Luther King Jr.
kids.nationalgeographic.com/explore/history/martin-luther-king-jr
This website from *National Geographic Kids* presents facts about Martin Luther King Jr.'s life and legacy.

Publisher's note to educators and parents: Our editors have carefully reviewed these websites to ensure that they are suitable for students. Many websites change frequently, however, and we cannot guarantee that a site's future contents will continue to meet our high standards of quality and educational value. Be advised that students should be closely supervised whenever they access the Internet.

INDEX

A
activism, 7, 12, 13, 20, 21, 27
Alabama, 7, 8, 10, 11, 12, 13
apartheid, 26, 27
assassinations, 19, 20, 28

B
books, 23, 25, 27, 28
Boston, Massachusetts, 11, 12

C
children, 11, 14, 18
Civil Rights Act of 1964, 21, 28

F
Freedom Concerts, 17, 18

I
India, 14

J
Jim Crow laws, 6

K
King Center, 23, 24

L
LGBTQ+ community, 24

M
Martin Luther King Jr. Day, 23, 24, 28
Montgomery bus boycott, 7, 13, 15
music, 11, 12, 18

P
Parks, Rosa, 7
Poor People's Campaign, 20

S
segregation, 6, 8, 9, 10, 11, 13, 15, 21, 26, 27
Southern Christian Leadership Conference, 17

V
Voting Rights Act of 1965, 21
voting rights, 5, 21

W
Women's International League for Peace and Freedom, 19
Women's Strike for Peace, 19